Contents

Language Arts

Sentence Naming Part	6
Nouns	10
Punctuation	12
Proper Nouns	18
Adjectives	19
Forming Adjectives	20
Compound Words	21
Plural Nouns	28
Rhyming Words	32
Alphabetical Order	36
Capitalization	38
Fact or Opinion	46
Antonyms and Synonyms	50
Homonyms	51
Captions	54
Activities to Share	57

Mathematics

Calendar	4
Addition/Subtraction Story Problems	13
Fractions	14
Addition/Subtraction	15
Coin Values	25
Perimeter and Shapes	26
Addition/Subtraction	29
Place Value	30
Estimate Measures	31
Fact Families	37
Days of the Week	39
Elapsed Time	40
Patterns in Time	41
Addition	42
Bar Graphs	44
Shapes	45
Skip Counting by Twos	47
Fractions	52
Math Puzzle	53
Activities to Share	60

Science

Signs of the Seasons	2
Summer Weather	3
Classification	7
Plant Parts	8
Weather Definitions	22
Reading Thermometers	23
Weather Crossword	24
Weight Comparison	43
Plant Life Cycle	48
Butterfly Life Cycle	49
Activities to Share	58

Social Studies

Past and Present	16
How Work Has Changed	17
Transportation	33
Map and Map Key	34
Activities to Share	59

Recommended Reading	55
Answers	61

© 2000 School Zone Publishing Company

Signs of the Seasons

Signs of the season happen in nature.
Some signs are made by what people do.
Write Spring, Summer, Fall, or Winter under the correct picture.

1. _____

2. _____

3. _____

4. _____

2 Signs of the Seasons © 2000 School Zone Publishing Company

Summer Days

Many words describe summer weather. Circle the words in the puzzle.

HOT SUNNY DRY
WET DAMP
WINDY BREEZY RAINY
DRIZZLY HUMID

```
H O S U N N Y T D
O M I N Y S D N R
T H U M I D N D I
R M A R A Z O R Z
B T R A I N Y Y Z
R W M A F D E U L
E I O D E Y D T Y
E N F A J P M K H
Z D A M K G T M D
Y Y D P O B W E T
```

Write four words that describe a good day to go to the beach.

_____ _____
_____ _____

Time in a Line

A time line is a good way to show the order in which things happen.

The top time line shows the seasons.
The bottom time line shows the months of the year.

1. January is in what season? _____

2. July is in what season? _____

3. Name a fall month. _____

4   Calendar   © 2000 School Zone Publishing Company

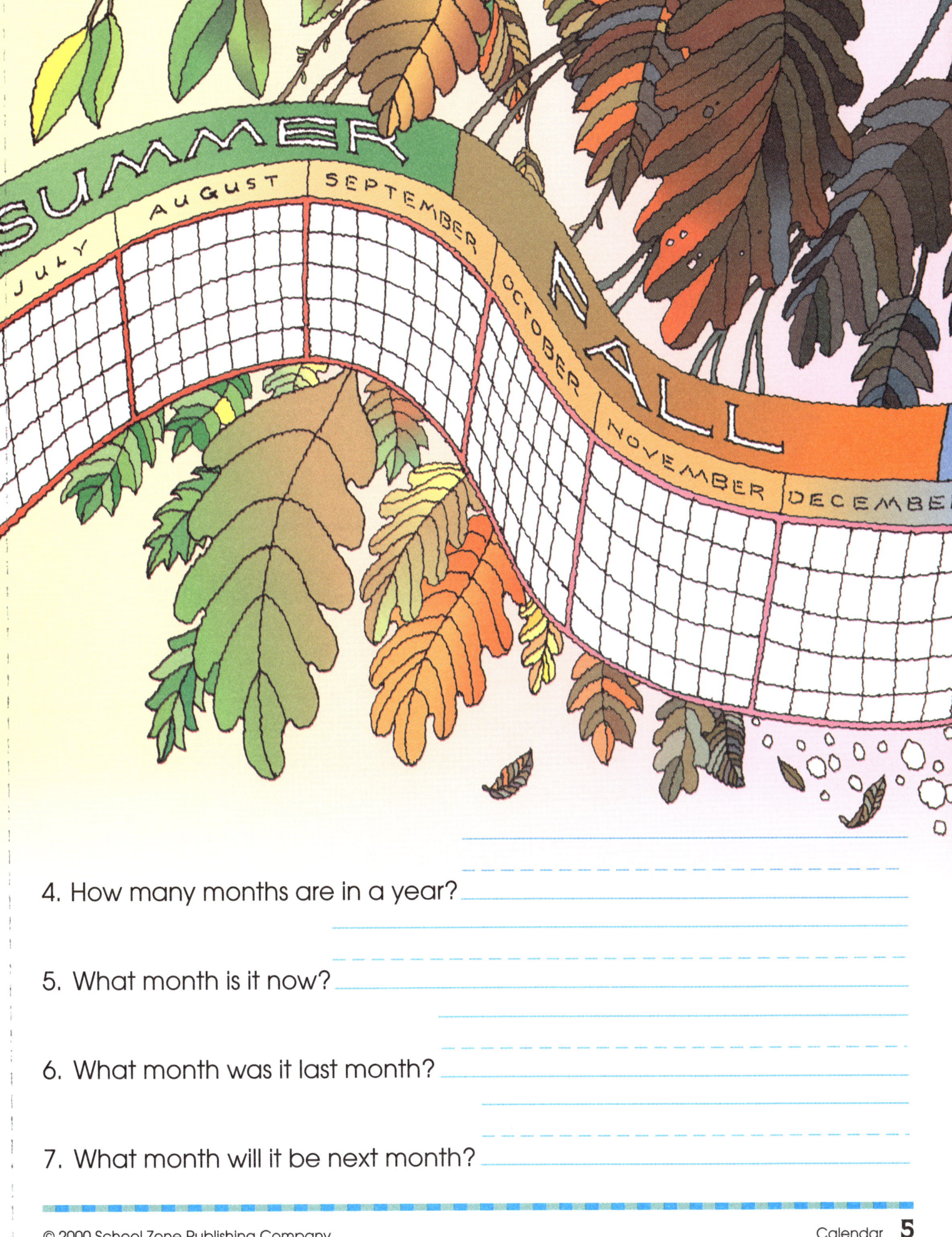

4. How many months are in a year? _____

5. What month is it now? _____

6. What month was it last month? _____

7. What month will it be next month? _____

A Summer Garden

This picture shows a garden in summer.

- A sentence has a **naming part**. The naming part tells who or what the sentence is about.
- The **family** is in the garden. **Who**
- **Flowers** are in bloom. **What**

Underline the naming part for each sentence. Then tell if it names **who** or **what**. Write **who** or **what** on the line.

1. Father picks some tomatoes.

2. Mother waters the flowers.

3. The corn grows tall.

4. The carrots are big.

Sentence Naming Part

Time to Pick

Some things in the garden are ready to pick.

Draw a line from each word to the basket where it belongs.

| tulips | melon | corn | grapes |
| peppers | beans | roses | cherries | lilacs |

Circle the three things in each group that are alike.

1. carrot   orange   bean   corn
2. hose   rake   shovel   plant
3. leaf   green   stem   root
4. lake   pond   hill   river
5. moon   day   month   year
6. fly   worm   bee   mosquito

Summer Foods Are Delicious

In summer, many plants grow fast. Most plants make their own food. They need air, sunlight, and water.

Fruit is the part of a plant that contains the seeds. Some plant seeds dot the outside of the fruit.

People eat different parts of plants.
Write the name of the plant part we eat.

1. People eat the _____ of some plants.

2. People eat the _____ of some plants.

3. People eat the _____ of some plants.

8 Plant Parts   © 2000 School Zone Publishing Company

Draw your favorite food from a plant. What part is it?

4. People eat the _____ of some plants.

5. People eat the _____ of some plants.

6. People eat the _____ of some plants.

Let's Go for a Swim!

These words name things you see at the beach.

girls   book   ball   baby   rocks   Waves

Naming words are called nouns. A **noun** names a person, an animal, a place, or a thing.

Write a noun from the box to finish each sentence.

1. Some boys and _____ are swimming.

2. A big, red _____ floats in the water.

3. A woman is reading a _____ .

4. A blue and white umbrella shades a _____ .

5. _____ splash over the _____ .

10   Nouns   © 2000 School Zone Publishing Company

Write two sentences about the beach.
Underline the nouns.

Circle three nouns in each row.
One word is not a noun.

6. pail   snail   fail   tail

7. shell   bell   well   tell

A Day at the Beach

Punctuation Marks
- Use a **period** (.) to end a sentence that tells.
- Use a **question mark** (?) to end a sentence that asks.
- Use an **exclamation mark** (!) to end a sentence that shows surprise or strong feelings.

A **sentence** is a group of words that tells a complete thought. A sentence begins with a capital letter. A sentence ends with a punctuation mark.

Write a sentence with each group of words. Write them in an order that makes sense.

1. sand Amy in plays the

2. a find seashell Patty Does

3. in Peter pail his sand puts

4. water Brr! cold The is

5. caught ball the Rex

Picnic at the Beach

Add or subtract to find the answer to each story problem.

1. Uncle Jim brought 12 cans of juice. He drank 6. How many does he have left?

   _____ − _____ = _____ cans of juice

2. There are 15 eggs on a plate. If people eat 7 of them, how many will be left?

   _____ − _____ = _____ eggs

3. Mother cooked 13 hot dogs. Then she cooked 5 more hot dogs. How many did she cook?

   _____ + _____ = _____ hot dogs

4. Aunt Mary brought cookies. Eight cookies are on a plate. Eight more are in the box. How many cookies did Aunt Mary bring?

   _____ + _____ = _____ cookies

5. Thirteen people want watermelon. Father cut 6 slices. How many more does he need to cut?

   _____ − _____ = _____ slices

Beach Towels

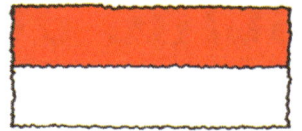

1 part shaded
2 parts in all
1/2

Each towel has a different design.
How many parts of the whole are colored?
Circle the correct fraction.

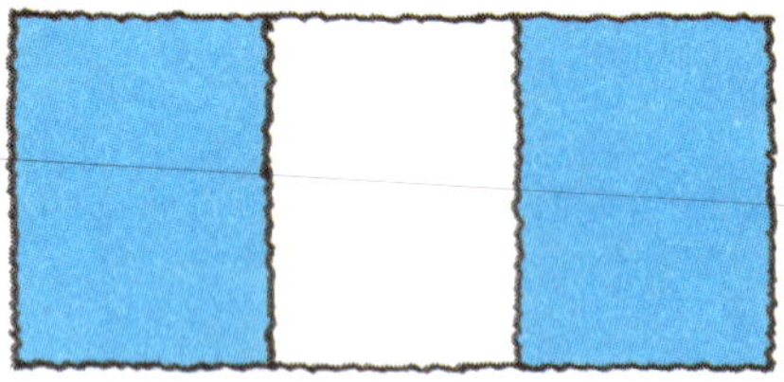

1/3   2/3

3/4   3/6

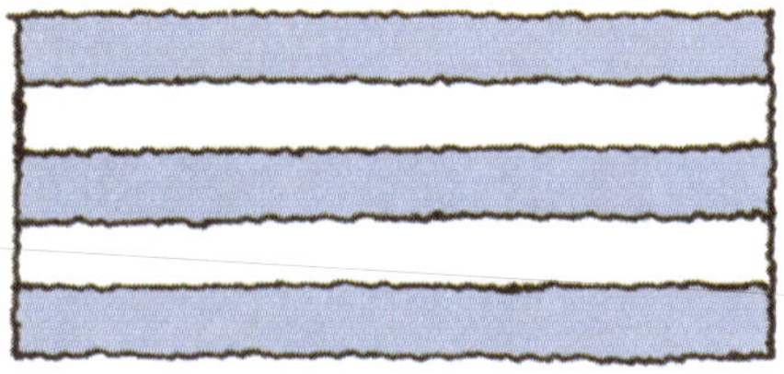

3/5   2/5

2/4   1/3

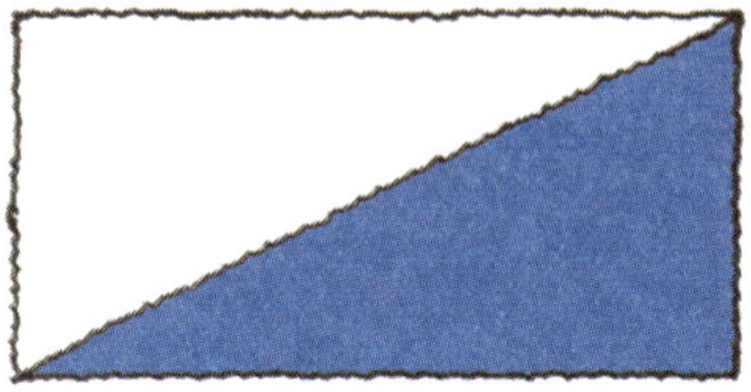

1/4   1/2

4/6   4/8

Color to show the fraction.

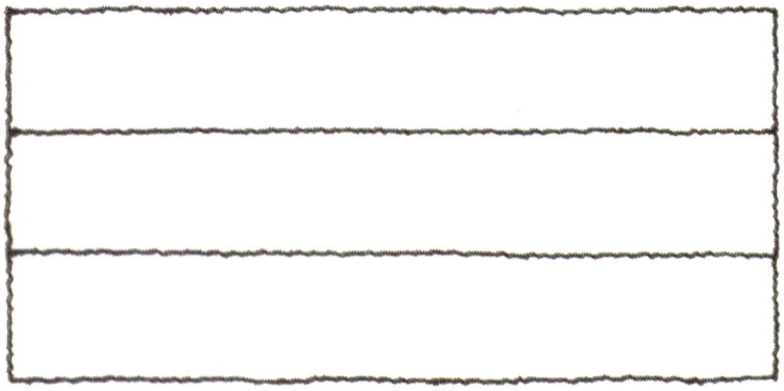

2/3

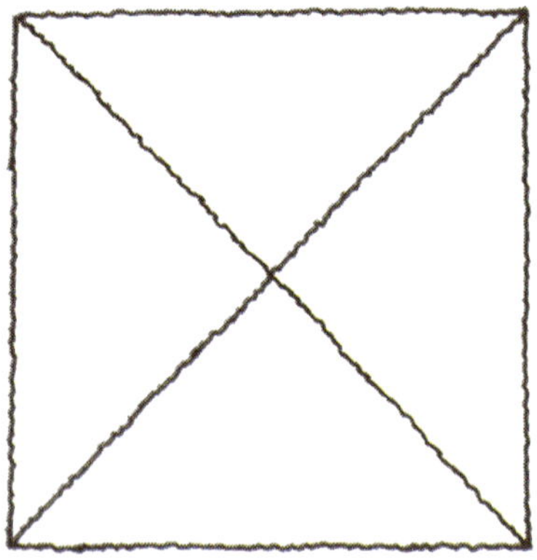

2/4

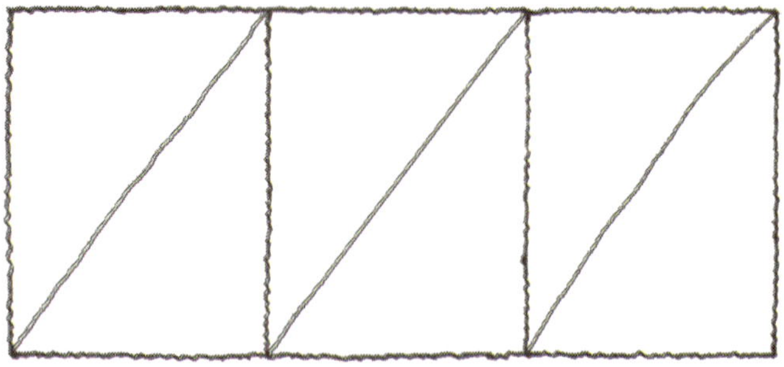

3/6

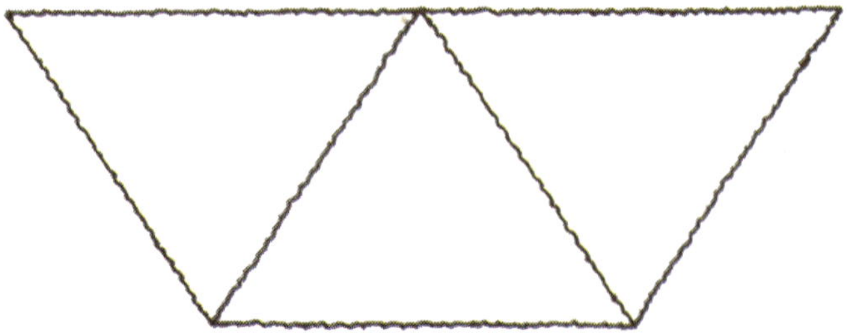

1/3

14 Fractions

© 2000 School Zone Publishing Company

Whirling Wheels

Add to finish these number wheels.

Subtract to finish these number wheels.

Addition/Subtraction 15

One Hundred Years Ago

Even 100 years ago, people liked the beach. There are now new things to do at the beach.

Circle three things that are new. ✓ three that people did 100 years ago.

16 Past and Present

© 2000 School Zone Publishing Company

Yesterday and Today

Some work has also changed over time. Some has stayed the same. Draw a line to show how work was once done to how it has changed.

What has stayed the same? ✓ the picture.

100 Years Ago **Today**

Fun Months

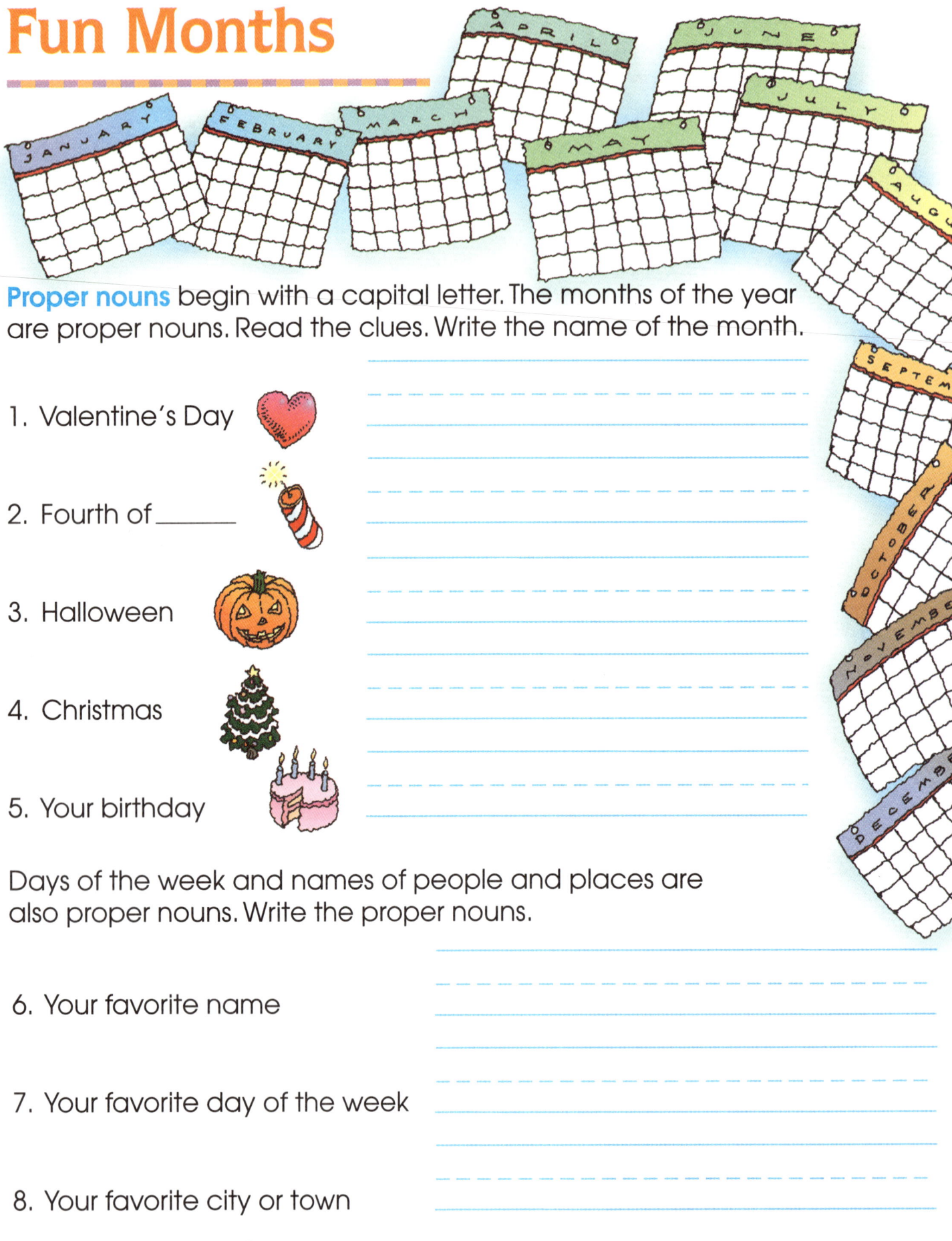

Proper nouns begin with a capital letter. The months of the year are proper nouns. Read the clues. Write the name of the month.

1. Valentine's Day

2. Fourth of _____

3. Halloween

4. Christmas

5. Your birthday

Days of the week and names of people and places are also proper nouns. Write the proper nouns.

6. Your favorite name

7. Your favorite day of the week

8. Your favorite city or town

A Parade of Adjectives!

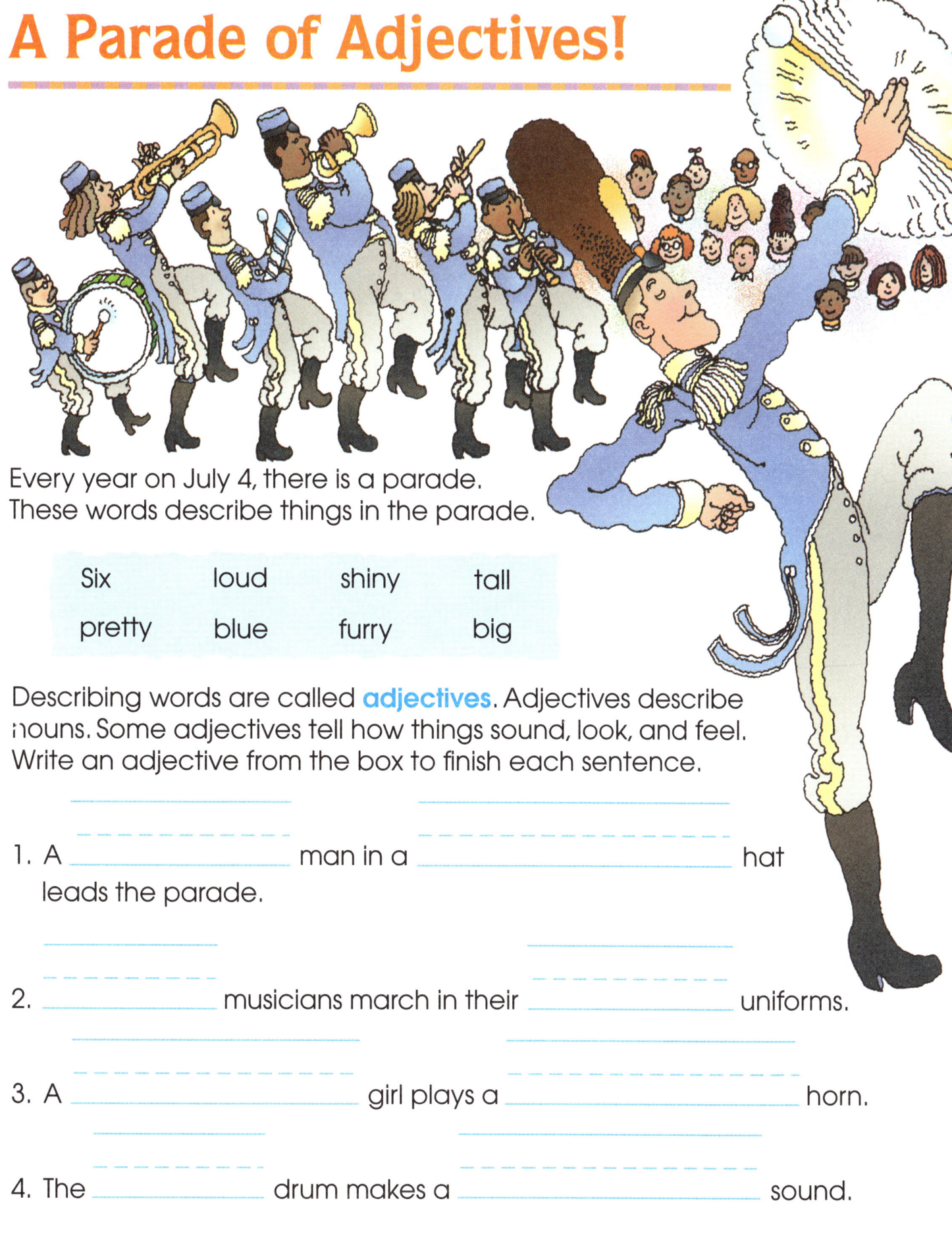

Every year on July 4, there is a parade. These words describe things in the parade.

Six	loud	shiny	tall
pretty	blue	furry	big

Describing words are called **adjectives**. Adjectives describe nouns. Some adjectives tell how things sound, look, and feel. Write an adjective from the box to finish each sentence.

1. A _____ man in a _____ hat leads the parade.

2. _____ musicians march in their _____ uniforms.

3. A _____ girl plays a _____ horn.

4. The _____ drum makes a _____ sound.

High, Higher, Highest

Write the adjective using **er** or **est**.

1. Debby's baton is (high) than Gail's.

2. Perri's baton is the (high) of all three.

3. The (smooth) twirler on the team is Gail.

4. Debby is a (fast) twirler than Perri.

5. Perri is (old) than Debby.

6. Gail is the (young) of all.

- Add **er** to some adjectives to compare two people, animals, places, or things.
- Add **est** to some adjectives to compare more than two nouns.

Compound Words

Sometimes two words are joined together to make a new word.
    The parade lasted all **afternoon**.
    after + noon = afternoon
A word that is made by joining two words is a **compound word**.

Read the story. Underline each compound word. Then write the two words that make the compound word.

Tracy and her family went downtown to watch the parade. They found a good spot between the playground and the schoolhouse. It was a hot day. They were standing outside in the sun for a long time. Luckily, the fireworks were at nighttime. So Tracy and her family cooled off in the evening.

1. _____ + _____

2. _____ + _____

3. _____ + _____

4. _____ + _____

5. _____ + _____

6. _____ + _____

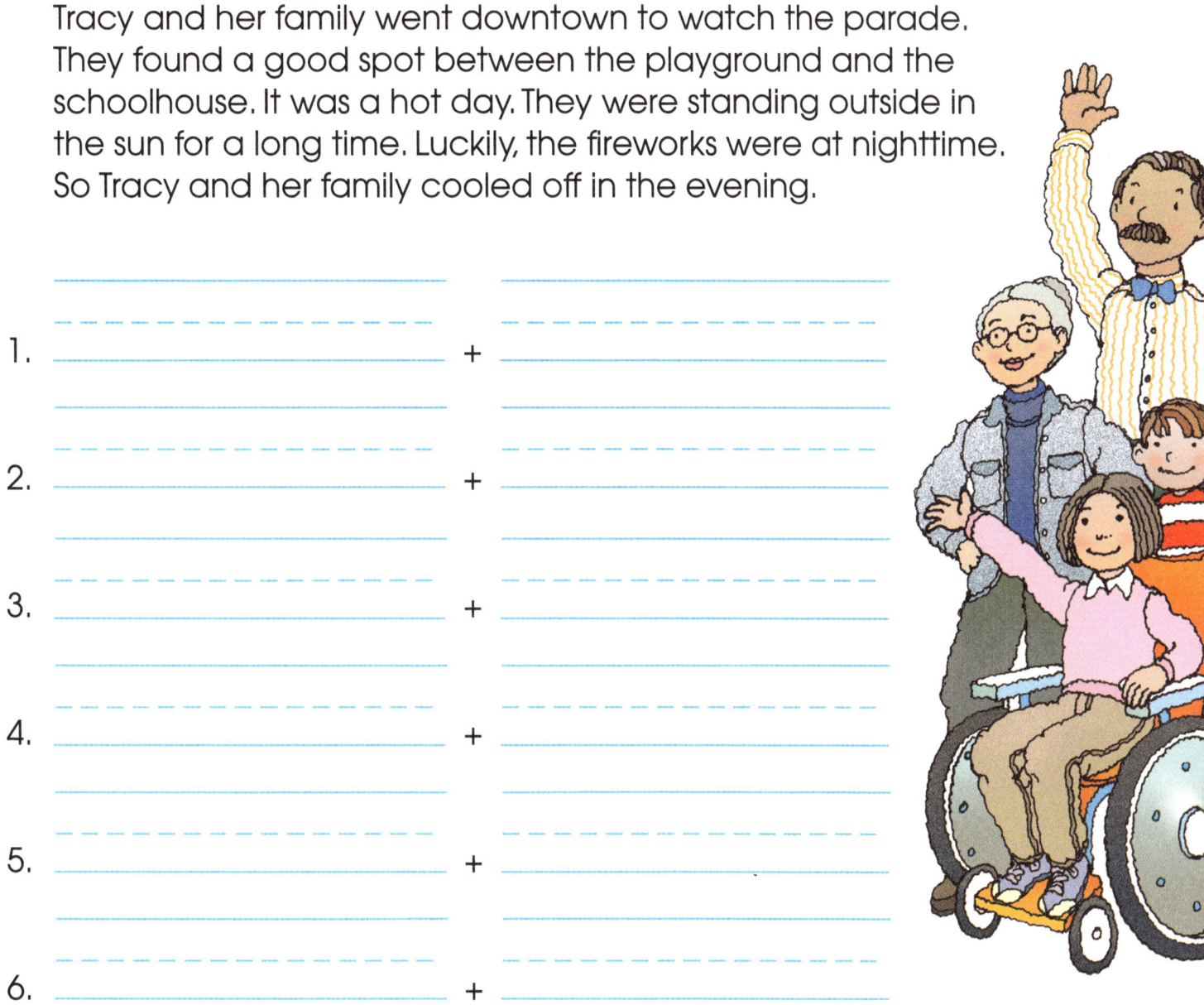

Dress for the Weather

Weather changes from day to day. Weather also changes with the seasons.

A **thermometer** measures temperature. The warmer the weather, the higher the liquid in a thermometer rises. Temperature is measured in degrees. These thermometers go up and down by two-degree steps from -10°.

- **Weather** is made up of temperature, precipitation, and wind speed.
- **Temperature** tells how hot or cold the air is.
- **Precipitation** is water in the form of rain, snow, sleet, or hail.
- **Wind** is moving air.

This thermometer says 32°, the temperature at which water freezes. It's cold!

This thermometer says 76°. Shorts can be worn on this warm day.

This thermometer says 56°. It's cool today. A sweater feels good.

22 Weather Definitions

© 2000 School Zone Publishing Company

Summer, Fall, Winter, and Spring

Read the thermometers. Write each temperature in the box. Then draw a line from each child to the temperature for which he or she is dressed.

Reading Thermometers

What Makes Weather?

Write weather words to fill in the puzzle.

Across

1. What we wear depends on the _____.
6. Rain, snow, and hail are kinds of _____.

Down

2. The push of air on the earth is _____.
3. _____ is what happens when water turns to water vapor.
4. Cold air can't hold as much _____ as warm air can.
5. Moving air is _____.

wind
water
air pressure
precipitation
weather
Evaporation

Lemonade for Sale!

25¢

20¢

You have made some lemonade and cookies. You sell them to people in your neighborhood. Write the correct answer to each problem.

1. Tony buys 1 🥤 and 1 🍪.

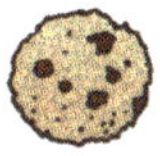

   What does he owe?   _____ ¢ + _____ ¢ = _____ ¢

2. He gives you 2 quarters.
   How much change
   should you give back?   _____ ¢ − _____ ¢ = _____ ¢

3. Jeanne buys 1 🥤 and 2 🍪 s.

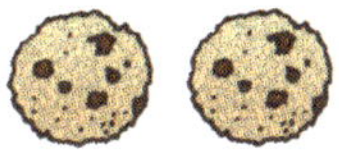

   What does she owe?   _____ ¢ + _____ ¢ = _____ ¢

4. She gives you 3 quarters.
   How much change
   should you give back?   _____ ¢ − _____ ¢ = _____ ¢

5. Brad has 1 💵.

   How many 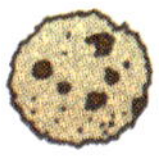  s can he buy?

   _____

25¢   10¢
5¢   1¢
= 🪙🪙🪙🪙

© 2000 School Zone Publishing Company

Coin Values   **25**

A Cool Pool

Swimming pools come in different shapes.
This swimming pool is a rectangle. It has four sides.
Count the units around the pool to find its perimeter.

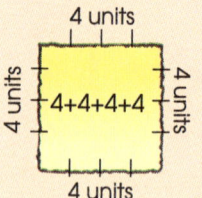

Perimeter is the distance around a shape.

The perimeter is 16 units.

Find the perimeter of each.

1. swimming pool _____

2. wading pool _____

3. sandbox _____

4. patio _____

5. Name the shape of the sandbox.

_____

_____

26 Perimeter and Shapes   © 2000 School Zone Publishing Company

PATIO

SANDBOX

6. Circle the one with the greater perimeter.

   sandbox   wading pool

7. Draw two towels on the patio. Make a red one 3 units wide and 4 units long. Make a green one 2 units wide and 5 units long. Find the perimeter of each towel.

   red _____

   green _____

More Than One

> To make more than one, add **s** to most nouns. Add **es** to nouns that end with **s**, **ss**, **ch**, **sh**, or **x**.

Study the pictures. Read the nouns.

pitcher

pitchers

peach

peaches

Make the noun in the ( ) name more than one. Then write the new word.

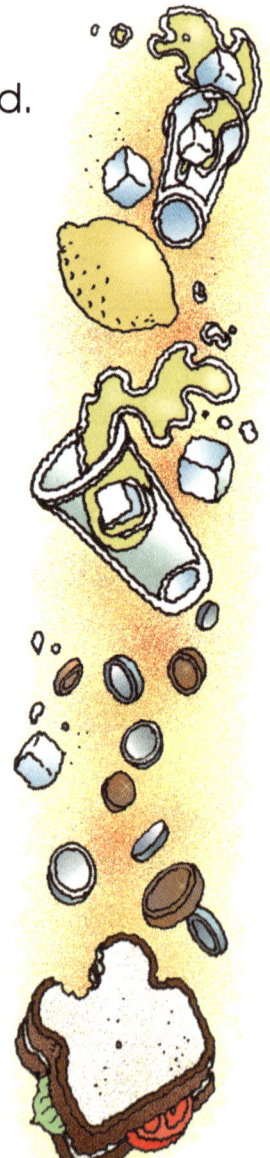

1. The children used three (box) to make a lemonade stand.

2. Mother gave them some (lemon).

3. She also gave them some (glass).

4. They need ice (cube) to keep the lemonade cold.

5. They also need (coin) to make change for customers.

6. The children ate (sandwich) and drank lemonade.

Who's in the Nest?

Help these math birds return to their answer nests! Write their names in the nests below.

The number is 2 greater than 10 + 3.

The number is 1 less than 2 tens + 8 ones.

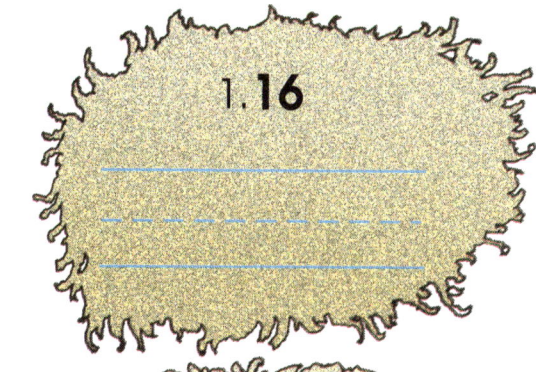

1. **16**

2. **13**

The number is 4 less than 4 + 0.

The number is 5 less than 9 + 9.

3. **27**

4. **15**

You say the number if you count by twos.

5. Which bird does not have a nest? _____

Addition/Subtraction **29**

Card Game

Use the numbers on the cards only once.

1. Find the greatest sum.

    5 8 4

2. Find the least sum.

    3 9 6

Use these cards. Write the greatest number you can. Write the least number you can.

		Greatest Number	Least Number
3.	4 1 9		
4.	8 2 7		
5.	6 3 5		

30 Place Value

© 2000 School Zone Publishing Company

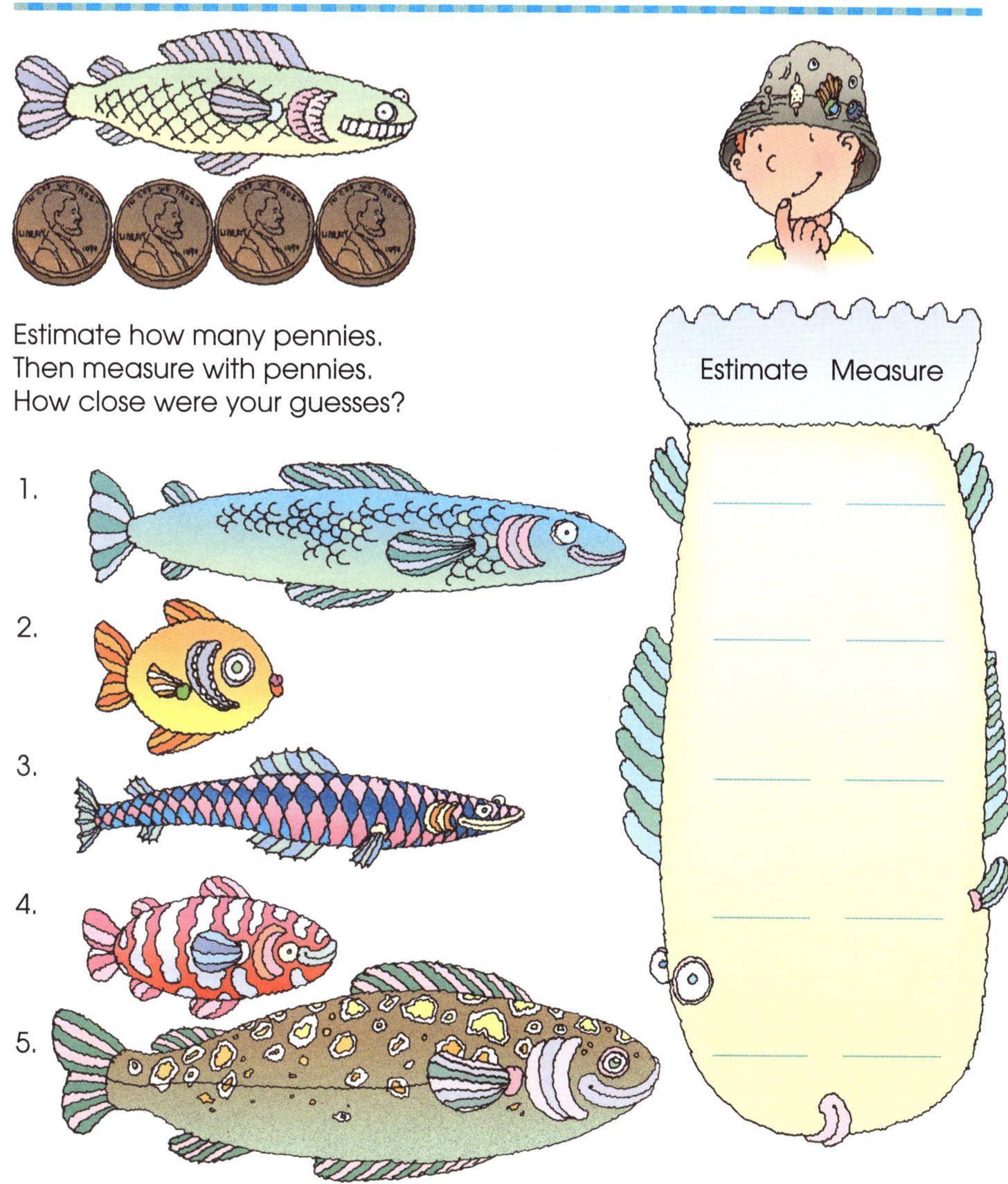

On the Go

Answer the riddles about ways to travel.
Then circle the words in the puzzle.

1. What word rhymes with slip?

2. What word rhymes with star?

3. What word rhymes with rain?

4. What word rhymes with us?

5. What word rhymes with pet?

```
S H P J E T E B
T P W A B T E U
R Z S H I P T L
A T R I L C B N
I C L B C A U I
N A I U A C A R
B U L S M U R P
```

Off We Go!

People get from here to there in different ways.
Look at the pictures. Write the words on the lines below.

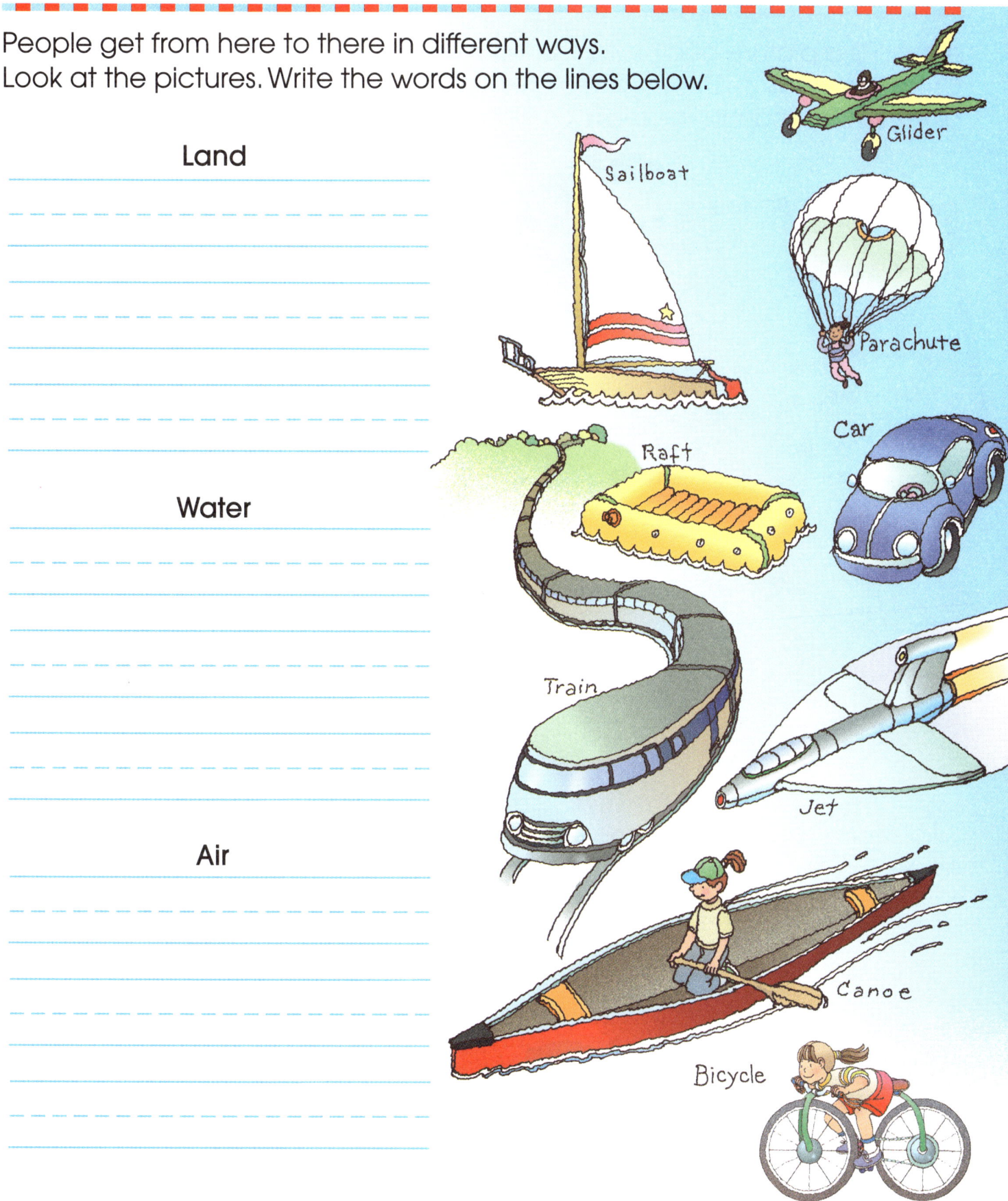

Land

Water

Air

Transportation

Crow River Camp

A map is a picture of a place from above. This map shows Crow River Camp. The small pictures on the map stand for different places in the camp. The map key tells what the small pictures mean.

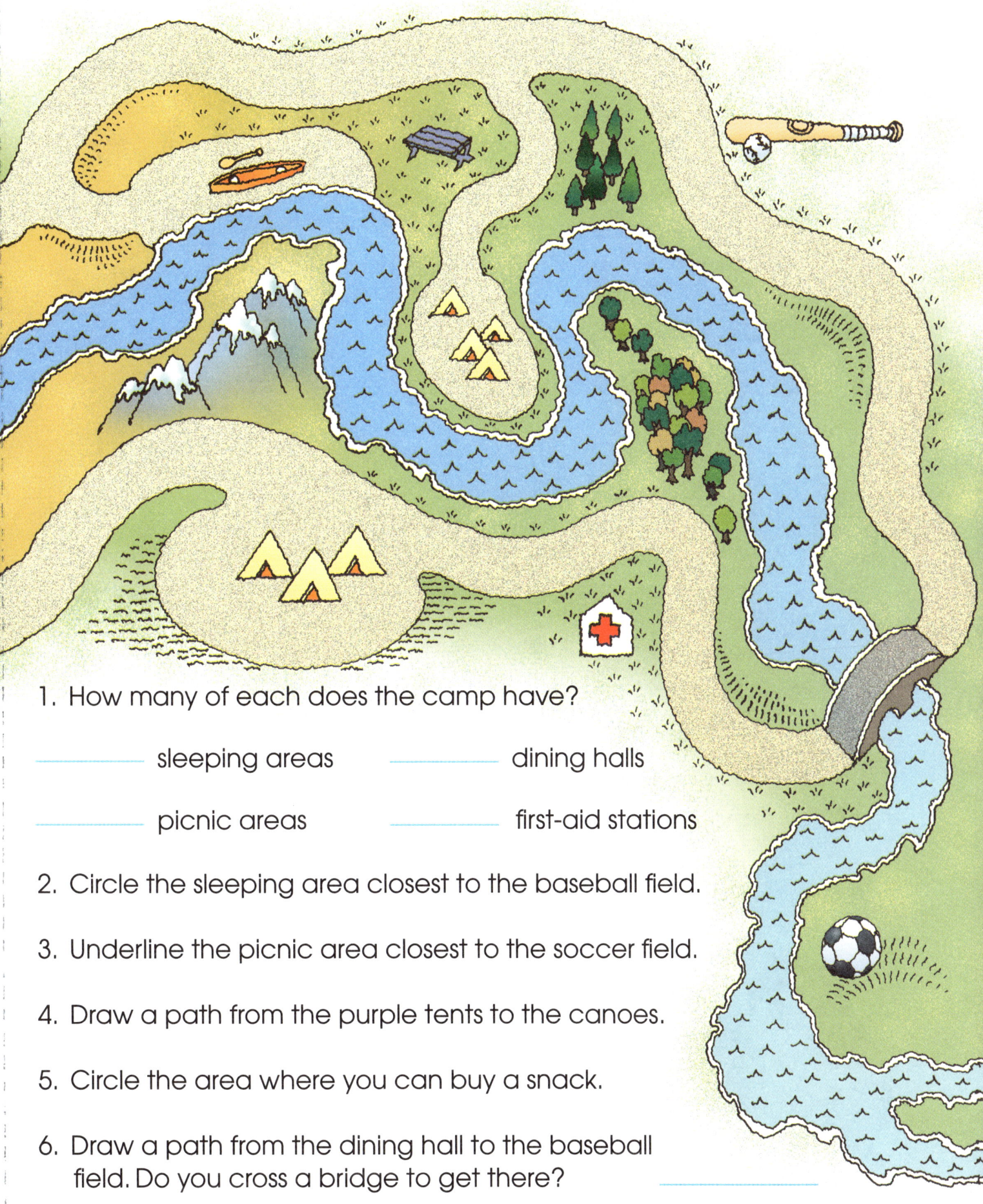

1. How many of each does the camp have?

   _____ sleeping areas   _____ dining halls

   _____ picnic areas   _____ first-aid stations

2. Circle the sleeping area closest to the baseball field.

3. Underline the picnic area closest to the soccer field.

4. Draw a path from the purple tents to the canoes.

5. Circle the area where you can buy a snack.

6. Draw a path from the dining hall to the baseball field. Do you cross a bridge to get there? _____

Map and Map Key

Bunkmates

ABC order is the order of the letters in the alphabet. Use the first letters of words to put them in ABC order.

    ant   **cat**   **pig**

The words *dig*, *dog*, and *day* begin with the same first letter. Use their second letters to put them in ABC order.

    day   **dig**   **dog**

Put the names of these bunkmates in ABC order.

1. Peter, Matt, Jamie

2. Lucy, Tina, Beth

3. David, Drew, Doug

4. Amy, Abby, Anna

36   Alphabetical Order   © 2000 School Zone Publishing Company

Postcards from Camp

Some children wrote postcards from camp. They forgot to use a capital letter to begin the name of a person, a pet, or a month. Find and circle each word that needs a capital letter.

Dear Mom,
Please pat my dog pat and say hello to him for me.
Love, Tim

Dear Dad,
A lucky girl named penny found a penny in the woods.
Love, Katie

Dear Grandma,
My best friend may come and visit me in may.
Love, Jon

Dear Kelly,
Next march, people from my camp will march in a parade.
Love, Carrie

Dear Aunt Sue,
The camp's dog freckles has spots that look like freckles.
Love, Chuckie

Admission Is Free

Monday Tuesday Wednesday Thursday Friday Saturday Sunday

The River Place Amusement Park is having free days. You must wear the right color shirt to get in free. Read the clues. Find out on which day you would wear each color shirt.

1. comes between Monday and Wednesday

2. comes between Wednesday and Friday

3. comes the day after Saturday

4. comes two days after Wednesday

5. comes the day before Sunday

6. comes a week after Monday

Time Gone By

Answer each question.
Show the time on each clock.

Ann's family arrived at River Place Amusement Park at 11:30 A.M. They ate lunch an hour later. What time did they eat lunch?

Ann's watch read 1:15 P.M. She and her family waited in line for a half hour at the Haunted House. What time did they get in?

The trip through the Haunted House takes 20 minutes. If you go in at 1:45 P.M., what time will you come out?

Clock Towers

River Place Amusement Park has two clock towers.
Characters come out at special times.
Write the time for each clock.
Draw the missing clock hands to complete the pattern.

1. Times to see

_____   _____   _____   _____

2. Times to see

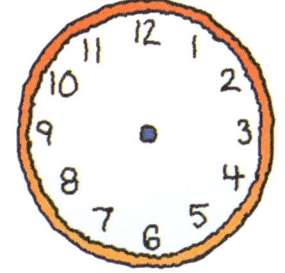   

_____   _____   _____   _____

Patterns in Time   41

Ring Toss

11-14 points
Rag Doll

15-18 points
Baseball

19-22 points
Bear

23-30 points
Lion

Each player can toss three rings.
Add each player's points.
Name the prize each player wins.

1. 7 + 7 + 6 = _____

prize _____

2. 6 + 7 + 3 = _____

prize _____

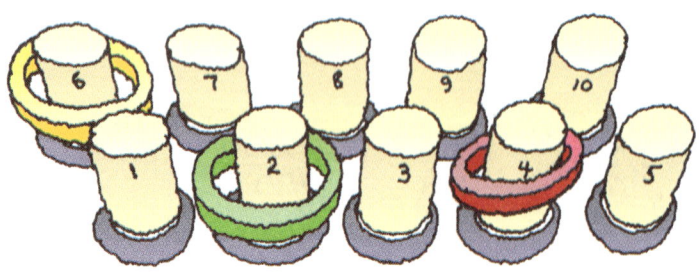

3. 6 + 2 + 4 = _____

prize _____

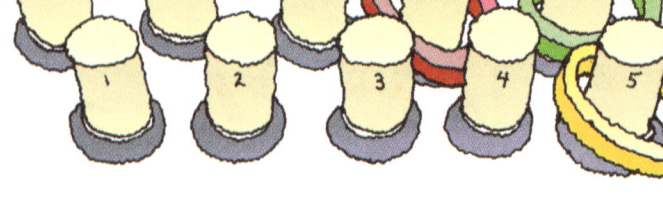

4. 10 + 9 + 5 = _____

prize _____

Light or Heavy?

Circle the one that is heavier in each pair.

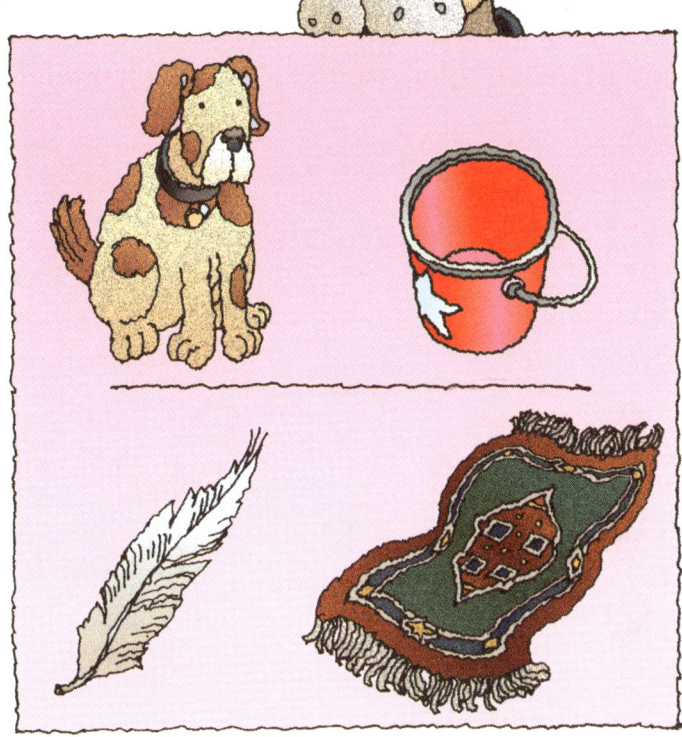

Circle the one that is lighter in each pair.

Weight Comparison

Ice Cream Cones

The Camp Snack Bar sells ice cream cones. What flavors of ice cream cones are liked best? Count the tally marks in the table.

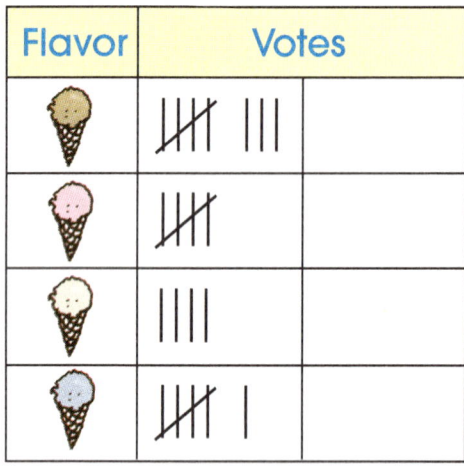

1. How many like chocolate best? _____

2. How many like strawberry best? _____

3. How many like vanilla best? _____

4. How many like blue moon best? _____

Fill in the bar graph with the information from the table.

Straw Shapes

Look at each set of straws.

Circle two shapes you can make with each set.

1.

2.

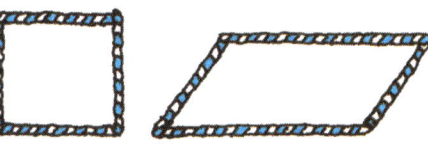

3.

4.

How many squares can you find?

_____ squares

Water Animals

A **fact** can be proved.
   Fish live in water.
An **opinion** is what someone believes.
   Fish are nice.

Write *fact* or *opinion* after each sentence.

1. Most ocean animals are fish.

2. Fish get oxygen through gills.

3. Fish make good pets.

4. Whales and dolphins are not fish.

5. Everyone should eat fish.

6. Fish have backbones.

7. Ocean fish are better than river fish.

8. Fishing is a good sport.

Find the Way Home

Help the sea horse find its way home. Start at 12 and count by 2s.

Skip Counting by Twos

Nature Cycles

Most plants and animals live through cycles. Here is the life cycle for a tree.

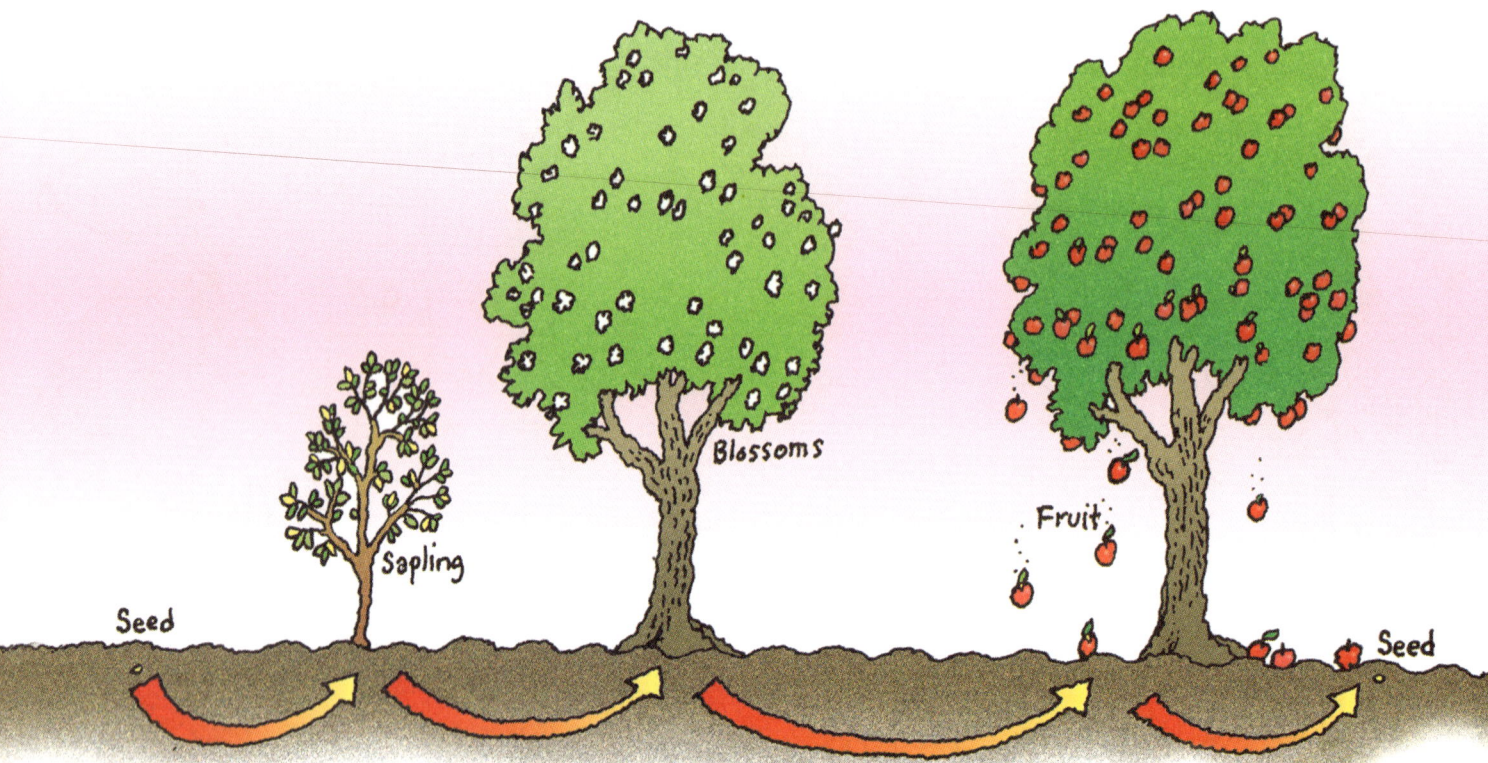

Write the missing word.

1. A tree begins as a _____.

2. Next, it becomes a _____.

3. A mature tree produces _____.

4. The blossoms become _____.

5. The fruit drops _____s.

48 Plant Life Cycle   © 2000 School Zone Publishing Company

Every butterfly goes through four stages during its life cycle:

1. egg
2. larva (caterpillar)
3. pupa (chrysalis)
4. adult (butterfly)

During each stage, the insect looks different and lives in a new way. Only the caterpillar and the adult can move about.

Write the missing word.

1. A butterfly begins as an _____.

2. The egg hatches into a _____.

3. The caterpillar turns into a _____.

4. A _____ breaks out of the pupa.

Butterfly Life Cycle

Bumper Cars

On the chart, write a word from a bumper car that means the same or opposite.

	same	opposite
glad		
noisy		
little		
quick		

50 Antonyms and Synonyms

Sound-alikes

Some words sound alike, but they have different spellings and meanings. Write the correct word to finish the sentences.

1. The _____ girls are going _____ town.
   to   two   to   two

2. They _____ their bikes on a bumpy _____ .
   rode   road   rode   road

3. The girls will meet _____ mother when they
   there   their

   get _____ .
   there   their

4. They _____ she would bring them a _____ book.
   new   knew   new   knew

5. Mother said she would _____ the book _____
   by   buy   by   buy

   lunchtime.

Homonyms

Camp Crafts

The campers are doing crafts. They are making bracelets.

1. Steve has 10 beads on his string. Circle the fraction that tells what part of his bracelet is red.

    1/2   **1/3**   **1/4**

    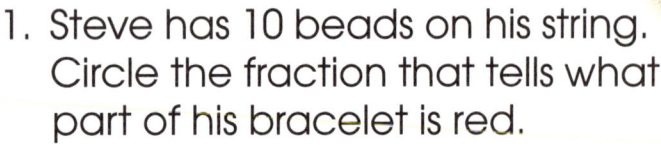

2. Pam has 9 beads on her string. Circle the fraction that tells what part of her bracelet is purple.

    1/2   **1/3**   **1/4**

3. Three children share 12 green beads equally. Circle how many each child has. Then circle the fraction that tells what part that is.

    1/2   **1/3**   **1/4**

4. Color 2/5 of these beads red.

5. Color 3/4 of these beads blue.

It's a Puzzle!

Look at the clues and solve the problems. Write the answers in the puzzle.

ACROSS

A. 2 more than 8
B. 105, 110, 115
C. 19 + 5
D. 21 − 8
E. 9, 12, 15
F. 3 tens, 8 ones
G. 120 − 15
H. 45¢ + 45¢
I. 40 − 27
J. 3 × 4

DOWN

A. 200 − 50
B. 20 − 9
C. 2 hundreds, 4 tens, 8 ones
D. 27 − 15
E. 2 × 9
F. 5 × 7
G. one dozen
H. $12.04 − $3.02

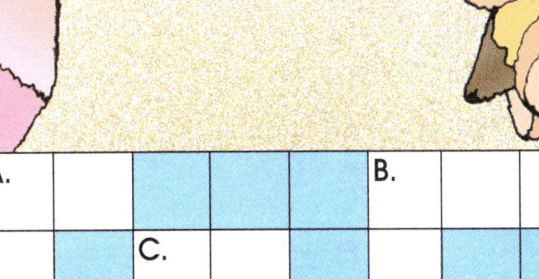

A Summer Album

A **caption** is one or two sentences that tell about a picture.

This is an album of summer fun. Write captions for the pictures. Tell what you like about each.

54 Captions

© 2000 School Zone Publishing Company

Recommended Reading

Aylesworth, Jim. **Old Black Fly**. Henry Holt and Company, Inc., 1992. A fabulous picture book using alphabetical order and rhyme to tell about the chaos a black fly causes one hot summer day.

Coates, Grace Dávila and Jean Kerr Stenmark. **Family Math for Young Children**. The Regents of the University of California, 1997. A book filled with interesting and fun investigations, activities, and explorations that children and parents can do together.

Deluxe Software. School Zone Interactive. Interactive software developed to teach, reinforce, and review skills in each subject area. Titles include **Math 1-2**, **Reading 1-2**, and **Spelling 1-2**.

Gibbons, Gail. **The Reasons for Seasons**. Holiday House, 1995. A simple illustrated explanation of what causes the seasons and why they continue to come again year after year.

Hall, Zoe. **The Apple Pie Tree**. The Blue Sky Press (Scholastic Inc.), 1996. Follows the changes in an apple tree through the seasons, showing how the tree plays an important part in the lives of some animals and children that depend upon it.

Kramer, Stephen P. **How to Think Like a Scientist**. Crowell, 1987. A practical book that encourages your child to use the scientific method.

Martin, Charles. **Island Rescue**. Greenwillow, 1985. In this adventure, the island is shown as a habitat in which people and animals are seen through a child's eyes.

Math Matters! Grolier Educational, 1999. A series of books written for children focusing on 13 important math concepts. Titles include **Numbers, Adding, Subtracting, Multiplying, Dividing, Decimals, Fractions, Shape, Size, Tables and Charts, Grids and Graphs, Chance and Average, Mental Arithmetic**.

Murphy, Stuart J. **Lemonade for Sale**. MathStart Series. HarperCollins, 1998. Four children need some money to fix up their clubhouse, so they open a lemonade stand. Readers are introduced to the concept of graphing as the children track their sales on a simple bar graph, showing the number of cups sold each day. Other titles in the series include **Too Many Kangaroo Things to Do, Divide and Ride,** and **Betcha**.

Recommended Reading, contd.

Ross, Kathy. **Crafts to Make in the Summer**. The Millbrook Press, 1999. Contains directions for 29 easy-to-make projects using materials that are easy to find in the summertime.

Scholar Books, School Zone Publishing Company, 1998. A series of workbooks that review and reinforce basic skills and knowledge. Titles include **Kindergarten Scholar, First Grade Scholar, Second Grade Scholar,** and **Third Grade Scholar.**

Steiner, Joan. **Look-Alikes**. Little, Brown, 1998. Parents and children alike will enjoy puzzling over the illustrations in this book, looking for more than 1,000 everyday objects cleverly hidden in plain sight.

Teague, Mark. **How I Spent My Summer Vacation**. Crown Publishers, 1995. On his summer vacation, Wallace Bleff heads out west to visit his aunt but is captured by cowboys along the way.

Teague, Mark. **Lost and Found**. Scholastic Press, 1998. Imaginative tale of Wendell, Floyd, and Mona, who find adventure when they get lost in their school lost and found.

Van Rynbach, Iris. **The Soup Stone**. Greenwillow, 1988. This folktale tells what people can accomplish if they work together.

If you live in the Philadelphia or Denver metropolitan areas or plan to visit, you can take your child to a United States Mint to watch money being made. The U.S. Mint offers free tours at these two locations. For detailed tour information, visit these Web sites: Philadelphia Mint at www.usmint.gov/facts/philadelphia.cfm or Denver Mint at www.usmint.gov/facts/denver.cfm

Your child can see pictures of antique postcards and stamps at the Web site for the Smithsonian National Postal Museum. Visit www.si.edu/postal for on-line exhibits, recent acquisitions, and collection highlights.

Activities to Share

Language Arts

Summer Riddles
Encourage your child to think about summer—its weather, plants, activities, and so on. Then take turns making up riddles about summer. For example, "I'm a summer flower. I have thorns. What am I?" Your riddles may be oral or written. If you write them, help your child use correct capitalization and punctuation. This activity will also reinforce listening skills.

Story Time
Provide frequent opportunities for your child to read throughout the summer months. You may want to have your child take part in a summer reading program at your local library. Help your child make and complete story maps about favorite books. Then have your child use the maps to summarize the books for you. A story map should be a chart with the following headings: Title, Author, Setting, Characters, Events.

Summertime
Challenge your child to see how many words he or she can find in the word *summertime*. You may want to post a large sheet of paper on the refrigerator or on a wall and invite your child to keep an ongoing list for several weeks. Encourage your child to check the spelling of words in a dictionary.

Picnic Words
Plan a picnic and ask your child to help you make a list of things you will need. After you have written the list, have your child identify the words that are nouns (plates) and the words that are adjectives (big). Then invite your child to add one or more adjectives to describe each noun. For example: old blanket; cheese sandwiches; big, red apples; cold, sour lemonade.

A Verb Game
Play a game in which family members take turns acting out verbs for each other to guess. Each verb must tell something that people like to do in the summer. Verbs might include swim, read, hit (a baseball), run, ride (a bike). Whoever guesses the correct verb first takes the next turn.

Sensing Summer
Invite your child to write a poem or a descriptive paragraph about summer using words that appeal to the senses. Tell your child that the poem or paragraph should describe what he or she sees, hears, smells, tastes, and feels in the summer. Encourage your child to brainstorm a list of ideas and sensory words. Then tell your child to choose the ones he or she likes best and use them to write the poem.

Activities to Share

Science

Watch for Animals
Take walks with your child throughout the summer to look for animals in nature. Have your child write the names of the animals he or she sees in a notebook. Reinforce your child's knowledge of animal groups by having him or her record the animals under appropriate headings: insects, birds, mammals, fish, amphibians, reptiles. Discuss the characteristics of animals in each group.

Safe Colors
Discuss the concept of camouflage with your child. Explain how color protects some animals because they match the background and their enemies cannot see them. Look for insects, birds, lizards, snakes, and toads hiding in the vegetation of summer: in the grass, among flowers, on branches, in leaves, or on tree trunks. Some butterflies, for example, have underwings that look like bark.

A Leaf Guidebook
Your child might enjoy collecting leaves from various trees in your neighborhood. Help your child identify the trees and put together "A Leaf Guidebook." Discuss the different kinds of leaves, simple leaf and compound leaf, and have your child arrange the leaves in the book according to type. If possible, include seedpods (fruit) in the book as well.

Plant Cycle
Demonstrate the life cycle of a plant to your child with a garden in a box. At the beginning of the summer, plant flower seeds in a flower box. Encourage your child to observe the plants as they grow and to note each phase of a plant's life. Help your child draw a labeled diagram of the life cycle of a plant. Use labels such as seed, seedling, leaves, bud, flower, new seeds, and wilting.

Moon Chart
Talk with your child about the different phases of the moon. Encourage him or her to observe the moon over the summer and record its phases. You may wish to compare your child's observations to a calendar that notes moon phases. Help your child make a "Moon Chart." Discuss the moon cycle, pointing out how the phases repeat.

Health Checklist
Help your child create a list of things he or she can do each day to stay healthy. The list might include such items as wash hands, eat a balanced diet, brush teeth, get fresh air, exercise, and get a good night's sleep. Encourage your child to check off what he or she remembers to do each day. You may wish to draw a happy face or put a sticker on the chart to acknowledge a "healthy week."

Activities to Share

Social Studies

Time Lines of Our Lives
Help your child make a time line of his or her life. Talk about important events and dates to include, such as when he or she was born, walked, talked, started preschool, started first grade, started second grade. Make a simple time line of important events in your life and share it with your child. You may wish to draw your time lines outside on a pleasant summer day, writing with chalk on a driveway or sidewalk.

Making a Map
Have your child make a map of one section of your town or city. Help your child take notes during a walk around this area. Encourage your child to notice the streets; kinds of buildings (stores, restaurants, public buildings); and natural areas (parks, flowers, ponds, lakes). As your child works on the map, remind him or her to label the streets and create a key with symbols for the different kinds of things shown on the map.

Talk about Talking
Introduce your child to the history of the telephone. Talk about today's phones and have your child find pictures of them in magazines and catalogs: push-button phones, cordless phones, cell phones, car phones, novelty phones. Then look in an encyclopedia together to see what phones were like in the past: dial phones, phones with no dials. Discuss how they are different from today's phones and how they are the same.

What Came Before?
"What Came Before?" is a card game you can play with your child during summer outings. Each player, in turn, takes a card, reads the invention, and then tells what came before it. Players get 1 point for each thing they name. Prepare several game cards by writing a modern invention on each one. Sample cards and answers include microwave oven (stove, fire), computer (typewriter, pencil), jet airplane (train, horse), TV (radio, newspaper).

Summer Trips
Point out to your child that many people take vacation trips during the summer. Explain that people go to outdoor places in different parts of America. Invite your child to make a "Travel Book" of these places by cutting out pictures from magazines. Have your child find examples of various landforms and bodies of water. Help him or her label pictures with geographical terms: mountains, plains, desert, island, peninsula, ocean, lake, and river.

My Park of the Future
Tell your child to think about an amusement park he or she has visited or seen on TV. Ask your child what he or she liked about the park. Then encourage your child to use his or her imagination and design a perfect amusement park of the future. Have your child create a name for the park, draw a plan of it, and tell you why it is a perfect amusement park.

Activities to Share

Mathematics

Math at the Store
Take your child shopping with you to the grocery store or drugstore. Encourage your child to read the price stickers of items under $5.00. Then name an amount of money and ask your child if it is enough money to buy the item. For example, if a pair of sunglasses costs $2.79, ask "Is two dollars and one quarter enough money to buy the sunglasses? Is three dollars enough?"

Math on the Street
Walk along a neighborhood street with your child and play "I Spy a 3-D Shape." The winner is the first person to find each of these shapes: sphere, cylinder, cone, cube, and rectangular prism. You may see the shapes in balls, streetlight globes, trash cans, fence posts, bird feeders, watering cans, ice cream cones, road-construction cones, birdhouses, doghouses, or cardboard boxes.

Math in the Kitchen
Invite your child to help you prepare individual fruit salads for members of your family. Give your child the opportunity to use fractions as both of you arrange fruits on each plate. Cut fruits into halves and fourths and have your child name the fractional parts. Encourage your child to divide fruits such as grapes, cherries, and strawberries into equal groups.

Beach Math
Use a visit to the beach to make up addition and subtraction problems for your child to solve. For example, ask your child to collect 18 shells, subtract the number that are pink, then tell you how many shells are left. You could make sand animals together, keeping track of how many pails of sand you use for each animal. Then have your child figure out how many pails of sand you used altogether.

Holiday Math
Have your child make a crepe-paper flag to decorate for Flag Day or the Fourth of July. Help your child draw the flag on a large sheet of paper, measure the length of each stripe, and figure out how much red and white paper you will need to buy. Then brainstorm ideas to determine how much blue paper you will need.

Math and Summer Activities
Encourage your child to make a schedule of things he or she will do on one upcoming busy day. Discuss that a schedule includes the name of each activity and the time each activity begins. Have your child read the finished schedule and tell you how long each activity will take. At the end of the day, compare your child's estimates to the actual time required for each activity.

Answers

Page 2
1. Fall
2. Spring
3. Summer
4. Winter

Page 6
1. Father - Who
2. Mother - Who
3. Corn - What
4. Carrots - What

Pages 8-9
1. roots
2. leaves
3. seeds
4. stems
5. flowers
6. fruit

Page 12
1. Amy plays in the sand.
2. Does Patty find a seashell?
3. Peter puts sand in his pail.
4. Brr! The water is cold.
   The water is cold. Brr!
5. Rex caught the ball.

Page 15

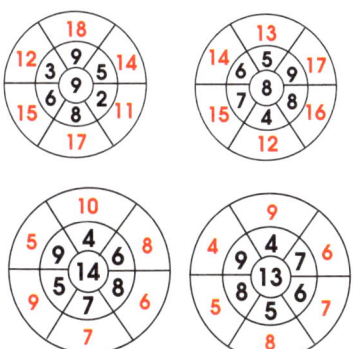

Page 3

Answers will vary.
hot   sunny
dry   humid

Pages 10-11
1. girls
2. ball
3. book
4. baby
5. Waves, rocks
   Sentences will vary.
6. pail, snail, tail
7. shell, bell, well

Page 13
1. 12 – 6 = 6
2. 15 – 7 = 8
3. 13 + 5 = 18
4. 8 + 8 = 16
5. 13 – 6 = 7

Page 16
Answers may vary.

Pages 4-5
1. Winter
2. Summer
3. September, October, or November
4. 12
5. Month will vary.
6. Month will vary.
7. Month will vary.

Page 7

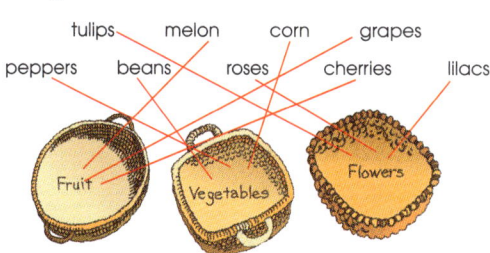

1. carrot orange bean corn
2. hose rake shovel plant
3. leaf green stem root
4. lake pond hill river
5. moon day month year
6. fly worm bee mosquito

Page 14

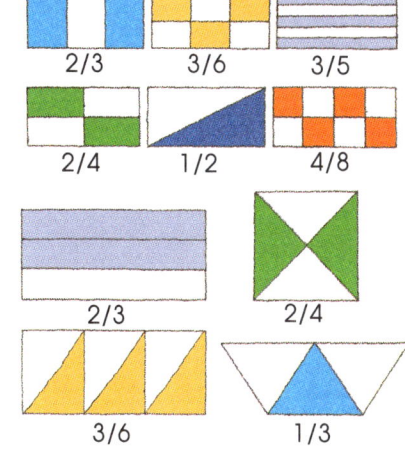

© 2000 School Zone Publishing Company

Page 17

Checked items will vary.

Page 18

1. February
2. July
3. October
4. December
5. Month will vary.
6. Name will vary.
7. Day will vary.
8. City or town will vary.

Page 19

1. tall, furry
2. Six, blue
3. pretty, shiny
4. big, loud

Page 23

Page 20

1. higher
2. highest
3. smoothest
4. faster
5. older
6. youngest

Page 21

Tracy and her family went <u>downtown</u> to watch the parade. They found a good spot between the <u>playground</u> and the <u>schoolhouse</u>. It was a hot day. They were standing <u>outside</u> in the sun for a long time. Luckily, the <u>fireworks</u> were at <u>nighttime</u>. So Tracy and her family cooled off in the evening.

1. down + town = downtown
2. play + ground = playground
3. school + house = schoolhouse
4. out + side = outside
5. fire + works = fireworks
6. night + time = nighttime

Page 24

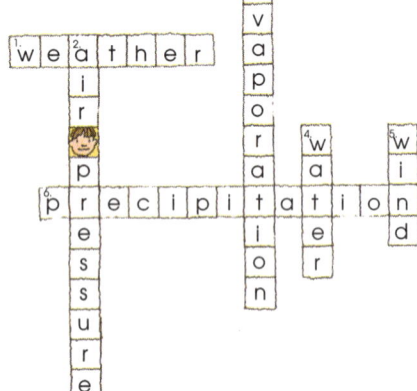

Page 25

1. 25¢ + 20¢ = 45¢
2. 50¢ – 45¢ = 5¢
3. 25¢ + 40¢ = 65¢
4. 75¢ – 65¢ = 10¢
5. He can buy 5 cookies.
   (20¢ x 5 = $1.00)

Pages 26-27

1. 30 units
2. 16 units
3. 21 units
4. 32 units
5. triangle
6. sandbox
7. red: 14 units
   green: 14 units

Page 28

1. boxes
2. lemons
3. glasses
4. cubes
5. coins
6. sandwiches

Page 29

1. 16 - Ben
2. 13 - Sue
3. 27 - Bob
4. 15 - Al
5. Joe

Page 30

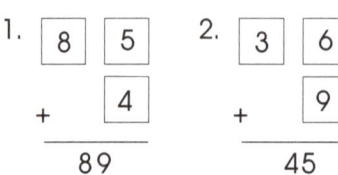

3. 941, 149
4. 872, 278
5. 653, 356

Page 31

1. 5.5
2. 2
3. 4.5
4. 2.5
5. 6.25

Estimates will vary.

Page 32

1. ship
2. car
3. train
4. bus
5. jet

```
S H P  J E T  E B
T P W A B T E U
R Z  S H I P  T L
A T R I L C B N
I C L  B  C A U I
N A I  U  A  C A R
  B U L  S  M U R P
```

Page 36

1. Jamie, Matt, Peter
2. Beth, Lucy, Tina
3. David, Doug, Drew
4. Abby, Amy, Anna

Page 39

1. Tuesday
2. Thursday
3. Sunday
4. Friday
5. Saturday
6. Monday

Page 41

1. 3:30   4:30   5:30   6:30

2. 1:00   1:15   1:30   1:45

Page 33

Land
bicycle
car
train

Water
canoe
raft
sailboat

Air
glider
jet
parachute

Page 37

1. 8 + 4 = 12
   4 + 8 = 12
   12 − 8 = 4
   12 − 4 = 8

2. 9 + 8 = 17
   8 + 9 = 17
   17 − 9 = 8
   17 − 8 = 9

3. 7 + 6 = 13
   6 + 7 = 13
   13 − 7 = 6
   13 − 6 = 7

4. 7 + 8 = 15
   8 + 7 = 15
   15 − 8 = 7
   15 − 7 = 8

Page 40

2:05

Page 42

1. 7 + 7 + 6 = 20
   Prize: Bear

2. 6 + 7 + 3 = 16
   Prize: Baseball

3. 6 + 2 + 4 = 12
   Prize: Rag Doll

4. 10 + 9 + 5 = 24
   Prize: Lion

Pages 34-35

1. 3 sleeping areas
   3 picnic areas
   1 dining hall
   2 first-aid stations

2. See blue circled area on map.
3. See underlined area on map.
4. See purple path on map.
5. See red circled area on map.
6. See green paths on map.
   There are two possible paths.
   Both paths cross a bridge.

Page 38

Dear Mom,
Please pat my dog (pat)
and say hello to him for me.
Love, Tim

Dear Dad,
A lucky girl named (penny)
found a penny in the woods.
Love, Katie

Dear Grandma,
My best friend may come
and visit me in (may.)
Love, Jon

Dear Kelly,
Next (march) people from my
camp will march in a parade.
Love, Carrie

Dear Aunt Sue,
The camp's dog (freckles) has
spots that look like freckles.
Love, Chuckie

Page 43

Page 44

1. 8
2. 5
3. 4
4. 6

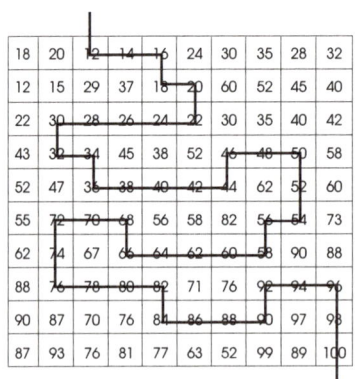

Page 45

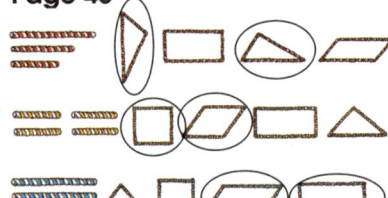

There are 10 squares.

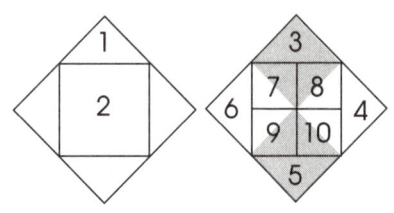

Page 46

1. fact
2. fact
3. opinion
4. fact
5. opinion
6. fact
7. opinion
8. opinion

Page 47

(number maze grid)

Page 48

1. seed
2. sapling
3. blossoms
4. fruit
5. seed (seeds)

Page 49

1. egg
2. larva
3. pupa
4. butterfly

Page 50

glad - happy, sad
noisy - loud, quiet
little - small, big
quick - fast, slow

Page 51

1. two, to
2. rode, road
3. their, there
4. knew, new
5. buy, by

Page 52

1. 1/2
2. 1/3
3. 1/3

4.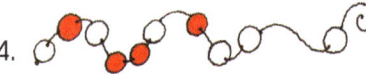

2/5 = 4/10 (color in 4 beads)

5.

3/4 = 6/8 (color in 6 beads)

Page 53

A.1	0		B.1	2	0
5		C.2	4		1
0		4		D.1	3
	E.1	8		2	
F.3	8		G.1	0	5
5			2		H.9	0
	I.1	3		0	
			J.1	2	

Page 54

Captions to pictures will vary.